Moritz Zieglmeier

The Potential of Wearable Technology in Amateur Football

A qualitative study

Anchor Academic
Publishing

**Zieglmeier, Moritz: The Potential of Wearable Technology in Amateur Football.
A qualitative study, Hamburg, Anchor Academic Publishing 2017**

Buch-ISBN: 978-3-96067-127-5
PDF-eBook-ISBN: 978-3-96067-627-0
Druck/Herstellung: Anchor Academic Publishing, Hamburg, 2017

Covermotiv: © pixabay.de

Bibliografische Information der Deutschen Nationalbibliothek:
Die Deutsche Nationalbibliothek verzeichnet diese Publikation in der Deutschen
Nationalbibliografie; detaillierte bibliografische Daten sind im Internet über
http://dnb.d-nb.de abrufbar.

Bibliographical Information of the German National Library:
The German National Library lists this publication in the German National Bibliography.
Detailed bibliographic data can be found at: http://dnb.d-nb.de

© Anchor Academic Publishing, Imprint der Diplomica Verlag GmbH
Hermannstal 119k, 22119 Hamburg
http://www.diplomica-verlag.de, Hamburg 2017
Printed in Germany

Table of Contents

List of Figures

List of Tables

1   Introduction

July 13th, Rio de Janeiro, Maracanã Stadium. The 118th minute of the World Cup Final between Germany and Argentina, when substitute Mario Götze scored the winner for the German team and achieved that the 24-year World Cup wait came to an end. From a fan perspective, the choice to substitute Mario Götze and not Lukas Podolski or maybe Julian Draxler seemed to be some mix of a good feeling by the coach and pure luck, but this substitution was based on much more than just gut instincts or a lucky thought. Head coach Joachim "Jogi" Löw and his coaching staff were using a wearable technology called "adidas miCoach Elite System" thanks to which they were able to find out that Mario Götze was the roster´s best overall player in playing and keeping the ball within short time and room on the pitch. According to the collected and evaluated data of the five-a-side football training units, Mario Götze provided the skills needed to win this game (Soper, 2015). However not only the German national team, also almost every other national team at this world cup, were using different kinds and brands of wearable technology during their training sessions to gather real time data from their players, which the staff could analyze to provide the coaching staff with an overview over specific strength and weaknesses of individual players in various situations which can occur on the pitch and to adjust the training sessions to improve how the staff wants each player to improve individually. (González, 2014) Apart from the 2014 World Cup in Brazil, almost every football club in the top European leagues and every Major League Soccer (MLS) franchise is using wearable technology for 3 to 4 years now, but this method of improvement in training session is nothing new in the world of sports, especially in the USA. Most football teams of the National Football League (NFL) are using wearable technology for years now in training and workout sessions as well as in league games to analyze the performances of their athletes and contribute with that to take the sport to a higher level every season (Johnson, 2015), (Neal, 2013).

While several wearable technologies made a huge impact on the training sessions of professional football clubs in the last years and are now a must have for every team which wants to keep up with the world elite, nearly no amateur football club is using this kind of technology in their weekly routine of training session. This thesis is going to examine the potential of wearable technologies in amateur football and will give answer to the following questions: How easy can wearable technology be used and is it a suitable method for amateur clubs in terms of functionality and usability as well as affordability.

All the above stated questions will be answered in this thesis to provide an evaluation concerning the potential of wearable technology in amateur football.

2   US sports as pioneers in using wearable technology

Before the use of different products of wearable technology in professional football and the potential for it to be used in amateur football will be discussed, there will be a short outlook to the United States of America, where the use of wearable technology is almost standard in training sessions as well in competitive games.

As described earlier, wearable technology is nothing new in US sports, especially in the big leagues outside of football like the National Football League (NFL), National Hockey League (NHL) and the Major Baseball League (MLB). The NFL teams are using a wide range of wearable technology for a long time now for many different functions. In 2013 Microsoft signed a contract with the NFL to provide all the teams with their Microsoft Pro tablet. This tablet is used on the sideline of a NFL game to be used by players and coaches to make it much easier for coaches to show their players which play from the team's playbook is going to be called next and which routes for each player will be chosen.

However, there are also technologies which are literally wearable and are used in training and also in games. Companies like Google or Oculus produced virtual reality headsets for team training in the NFL. These virtual reality headsets provide each player with a 360-degree camera to simulate specific in game situations and to work on them much more efficient. First used by the Dallas Cowboys, now a lot other NFL teams like the New York Jets and the Arizona Cardinals are using them to bring their training sessions to a higher und much more professional level. Also GoPro cameras are technologies that are being used by NFL teams, for example the New York Giants with their star player Odell Beckham Jr. This feature makes it easier for coaches to analyze the movements of their players and to give them individual advice to perform better in various situations. It also brings a positive side effect for fans to watch the actions of their favorite players from a point of view perspective. The NFL is also a forerunner in using wearable technology in real games, not just in training sessions. Apart from the Microsoft Surface tablets, which are not worn on the body by players, the NFL allowed the players to wear shoulder pad sensors for capturing live data like speed, body movements and GPS positions by the Illinois based company Zebra Technologies. These stats are a massive help for the teams coaching staff to quickly get individual information about their players and to adjust the playbook, the training sessions and the tactics individually to get a higher chance of succeeding in games. In 2015, for the first time the NFL allowed these chips to be inside the ball in a game to make it easier for the referees to spot the exact position of the ball after close plays and to measure the throwing speed (Plummer, 2016).

All these examples show that sport in the US, especially the NFL, is highly technological supported since some time now, even in league games, which is not applicable for football (Svetlik, 2015). However also the football teams kept up with the time, even if it took them a little bit, but they slowly recognized the advantages of bringing more and more wearable technologies into their training sessions.

3   Use of wearable technology in professional football

As described in Chapter 2, wearable technologies slowly made their way into football after being a success in other sports like American football, shown by the use of it by NFL teams. There are three big companies that made themselves a name in the market of wearable technology for football teams. adidas, STATSports and Catapult Sports. These three companies provide mostly every top team all over the world with their specifically developed wearable performance tracking systems. The components, functionality and which professional team uses which product will be exemplified in Chapter 3.

3.1   adidas miCoach Elite Team System

The probably best known product on the market for wearable technology in football, due to the worldwide popularity of the company, is the "adidas miCoach Elite Team System". This system, developed from 2010 to 2012 (MLS Communications, 2012) by German sportswear manufacturer adidas, provides the coaching stuff in training sessions with individual real time data from their players like speed, covered distance, heart rate, performance or acceleration. With the help of this data the coaching staff is able to identify the strengths and the weaknesses of every player so that they can efficiently impove training sessions and develop individual workout plans for players in order to increase their performance on the pitch.

3.1.1   Components and functionality

The system consists of five different components which are the "miCoach Elite Player_Cell", the "Techfit Elite Shirt", the "miCoach Elite Base", the "miCoach Elite Dashboard" and the "miCoach Elite Website" (Brüggen, Hübner, & Nationalmannschaft, 2014).

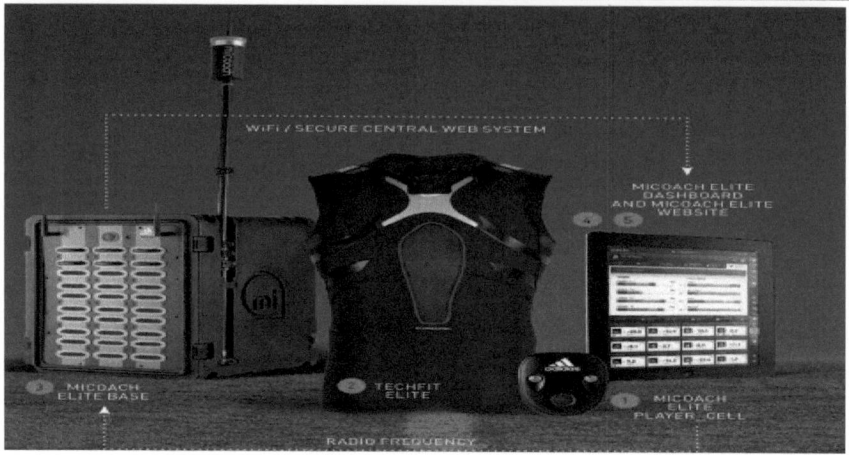

Figure 1: Components of the adidas miCoach Elite System
(Donath, 2012)

The "miCoach Elite Player_Cell" is a wearable sensor, which measures the real time data and transmits them via radio frequency to the "miCoach Elite Base". The sensor itself weighs only about 52 grams and fits in between the shoulder blades of the "Techfit Elite Shirt", which is a sleeveless compression shirt worn by the players. (Nosowitz, 2012) The battery of the cell lasts about 8 hours, so there should be no problem to collect a huge amount of data during long training sessions. (Vazquez, 2013) Apart from the included "miCoach Elite Player_Cell", the "Techfit Elite Shirt" measures the heart rate with inbuilt sensors while being comfortable to wear and it does not limit the movements of the players. The real time data from both the "miCoach Player_Cell" and the "Techfit Elite Shirt" will be transmitted to the "miCoach Elite Base", which is a portable, robust and water resistant receiver, placed on the side of the pitch. The "miCoach Elite Base" transfers the data to the "miCoach Elite Dashboard", a tablet for the coaching staff, with which the coaches are able to collect and analyze the individual real time data from each player. Based on the collected data, they are able to create new training schedules and training goals based on the data and to write summaries about recent training sessions. If the "miCoach Elite Base" is connected to the internet, the device automatically transfers all the data to the servers of the team to make it possible to review the data on the "miCoach Elite Website". Also the intensity of the training session, the individual level of fitness and the personal physical needs for each player will be displayed on the "miCoach Elite Website". Aside from the intention to make the training sessions more efficient for each player individually and to increase the performances, the "adidas miCoach Elite System" also contributes to the early prevention of possible injuries because the system captures the individual impact that every session had on a player, thus coaches can regulate the training intensity for some of them to prevent their bodies from getting injured and let them regenerate in the best possible way (Brüggen et al., 2014). The "adidas miCoach Elite System" was successfully launched on field during the 2012 "AT&T MLS All-Star Game" on July 25th in Philadelphia and was set to be part of every teams training sessions with the start of the 2013 season of the MLS (MLS Communications, 2012).

The "adidas miCoach" System also exists in a kind of "light version" for amateur athletes. In their online shop, the company sells the "adidas miCoach Smart Ball" and their "adidas miCoach X_Cell".

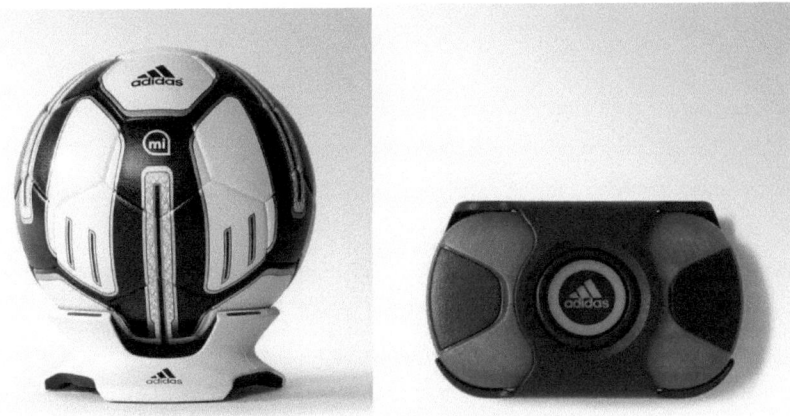

Figure 2: adidas miCoach Smart Ball and X_Cell
(adidas, 2016)

The "adidas miCoach Smart Ball" is a size five football with an integrated sensor which transmits data like speed, spin and flight path of the ball directly via Bluetooth to the "miCoach smart ball app" on the users Apple iPhone. The app allows the user to receive this information about his strike and provides feedback, tutorials and coaching tips how to perform bend, knuckle and power balls. The app also makes it possible to record the strikes of the user to help honing the technique and the skill set of the user. Another side feature is the possibility to share and compare the received stats with other users. adidas promises a battery life of about 2000 kicks per week with a charging time of only one hour, which makes it easy for the user to use the ball as often as possible (adidas, 2016).

The "adidas miCoach X_Cell" is a portable sensor which the user can strap around his body with an included textile strap. The function of this sensor is to measure the explosiveness of the user by collecting data about the quickness, reaction speed, intensity of play, jump height and heart rate and transmitting them via Bluetooth to the "miCoach" app on a smartphone. Referring to the collected data, the app provides the user with individual training cardio plans to improve endurance and quickness and also strength and flexibility plans to develop the users lower and upper body power. Another optional training plan are drills to improve jump height. Because the "adidas miCoach X_Cell" stores up to seven hours of workout data, the user is not forced to keep his smartphone while working out with the sensor (adidas, 2016).

3.1.2 Professional use

3.1.2.1 German national team

As mentioned in the Introduction, the German national team started using "adidas miCoach" at the 2014 World Cup in Brazil in their training sessions during the tournament and obviously the use of this system was a big success because the team won the World Cup in the final against Argentina after substitute Mario Götze scored the game winning goal seven minutes before the end of overtime (Brüggen et al., 2014). As also earlier described, the decision to substitute Mario Götze instead of another player was also relying on Mario Götze´s evaluated data in playing five against five, that was the best overall of the squad, in training sessions where it is important to keep control of the ball in a small space, to make quick decisions with little time, which was perfect for the situation in the final going into overtime (Soper, 2015). According to Darcy Norman, the director of EX-OS, a performance innovation company that partners with adidas and the German national team, the adidas miCoach system was used almost in every training session during the tournament to track and evaluate the performance of individual players of the German squad (Hymers, 2014). One of the key metrics, as reported by Norman, was analyzing the efficiency and fitness of players by tracking their production of power relative to their loss of energy during training sessions (Hymers, 2014). Another important aspect the team analyzed by using the miCoach system was the individual movement of players on the pitch in relation to their certain position. Referring to this data, the coaching team was able to set goals for each player, or a group of players with the same position on the pitch, which they had to achieve. Based on setting these specific goals for training sessions and position drills, the German national team created game plans for the upcoming match in the tournament and set up specially prepared training sessions in order to achieve the goals of the game plan (Hymers, 2014).

3.1.2.2 MLS teams

In the US-American Major League Soccer, the adidas miCoach system was standardized launched in 2013 to be used by all league teams during training sessions to gather individual player data and enhance team performance by using it. MLS franchise Portland Timbers noticed the value of evaluated data by the miCoach system some time earlier at the 2012 MLS Combine in Florida, when potential draft picks[1] showcase their talents in a process of several drill sessions. Some of these eligible players were outfitted with a miCoach sensor, including defender Andrew Jean-Baptiste, who eventually has been drafted by the Portland Timbers, after impressing them because of his outstanding measurements during a sprint session tracked with the miCoach system (Costello, 2012). Apart from relying on the adidas miCoach system during the MLS Combine, the franchise is also using the system during their training sessions but according to assistant coach Amos Magee, the coaching staff will not focus 100% on the evaluated data from the miCoach system and will still rely on their personal evaluation of players and their performance during a training session (Costello, 2012). He expressed himself on the homepage of the Portland Timbers:

"For example, just because a guy is covering a lot of ground, that doesn't necessarily mean it's smart running or that he's in the right place at the right time. That's a statistic that needs to come with experience. So some of these measurements are going to be useful, but some aren't. We'll just have to see which ones fill a void." (Costello, 2012)

Besides from the German national team and all the MLS franchises, several other professional football teams started adopting the miCoach system, among them Chelsea FC, one of the most popular football clubs in the world, five-time Premier League winner and Champions League winner in 2012 (Neal, 2013).

3.2   STATSports Viper System

Another well-known company on the market for wearable technology in sports, especially in football is STATSports Technologies Ltd. STATSports is a British company, founded in 2008, made themselves a name for developing the so called "Viper System", which let the company expand to places like Ireland, London, Chicago and Florida. The system includes

---

[1] College football players who signed up for the "MLS SuperDraft" to be picked by a MLS franchise after college

components which all together form a system for football teams to track and rate the performance of their players individually, similar to the "adidas miCoach Elite System". Apart from football, the Viper System is also used in sports like American Football, Rugby, Basketball and Athletics, so you can say the range of the company's various clients are very wide. The Viper System combines both software and wearable tools to form a sophisticated system to track a huge amount of data (STATSports, 2016).

3.2.1 Components and functionality

The flagship product of the Viper System and the so called "world's leading performance monitoring tool for elite sports teams on the market" (STATSports, 2016) is the „Viper Pod".

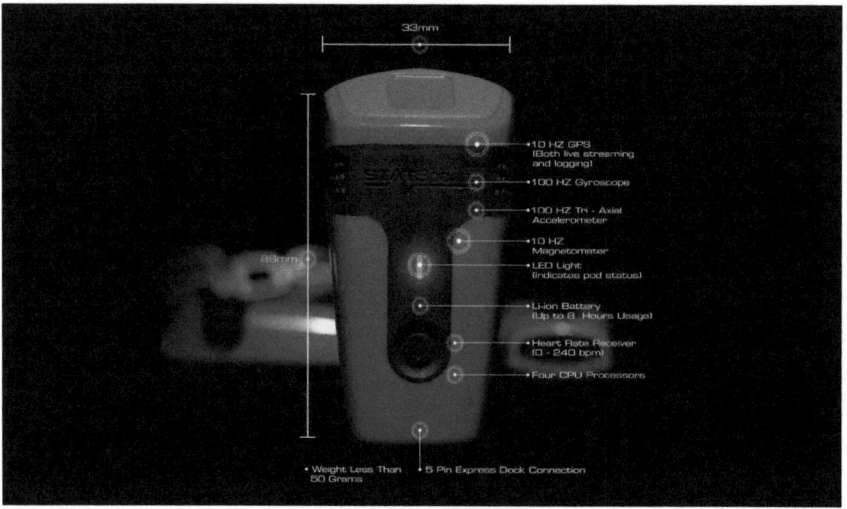

Figure 3: STATSports Viper Pod
(STATSports, 2016)

The "Viper Pod" is a high functional wearable sensor that streams live performance data in real time via the Viper Live Streaming software to be analyzed promptly or to log the data for post session download. The award winning unit stands out because of its ergonomically design, light weight (less than 50 grams) but nevertheless its high functionality including four processors, 3-D accelerometer, gyroscope and digital compass, an inbuilt heart rate receiver, a GPS module and its high streaming performance at a rate from 50 Hz (live streaming) to 100Hz (logging data). The inbuilt heart rate receiver is able to track both

10

heart rate variability and heart rate exertion from a range up to 240 beats per minute, so coaches can control the intensity of every training session for individually selected players. The Viper Pod unit is designed to fit in between the shoulder blade of players who have the choice of wearing a Viper Vest or a Viper Base Layer with or without sleeves. (STATSports, 2016)

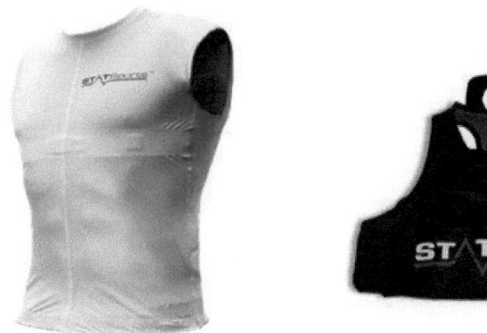
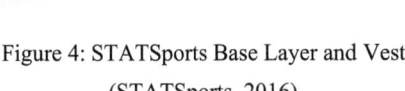

Figure 4: STATSports Base Layer and Vest
(STATSports, 2016)

Both of these products, the vest and the base layer are tight fitted and designed to always have a perfect GPS signal. In addition, the base layer contains an extra integrated pocket for the heart rate monitor so the player can wear it without a strap for better comfort. Other elementary components of the Viper System are the Viper Dock, the mobile antenna and the Training Ground Screen System. The Viper Dock is available with four or with twelve docking stations. The function is to download the data from the Viper Pods and to transfer them via USB to the STATSports software on the connected laptop where the coaches can evaluate them. The mobile antenna is sort of the "counterpart" to the Viper Docks, if a team decides to stream their training sessions in real time they are able to do this involving up to 30 players with the antenna. The advantages of streaming a training session live are that the coaching staff is able to intervene directly if they recognize something odd or un-satisfactorily during the session. By this time, several Premier League clubs have decided to install fixed antennas of the Viper system to their training ground, it is called the "STATSports VSI Smart Training Ground System" (STATSports, 2016).

3.2.2 Variety of possibilities

Now that there was given an overview of all the components of the STATSports Viper System, there will be an outlook to the entire features and functionalities this whole system is bringing to the table. The software which evaluates the data coming from the Viper Pod is able to split it up into a lot of various parameters. After receiving the real time data, the Viper Live Streaming software is able to provide information about individual speed, distance, acceleration, deceleration, heart rate variability, amount of sprints, dynamic stress load, high speed running and the high metabolic load distance. With this large number of player individual metrics, the Viper software offers a variety of different features to analyze, evaluate and eventually use them to improve each player and finally the whole team (STATSports, 2016).

One important feature for professional football teams that the Viper software offers is the possibility of injury prevention and giving an outlook to a players ongoing rehabilitation. By using the data received from the accelerometer, the system delivers information about the impact to the left and the right foot of the player in a pie chart (STATSports, 2016).

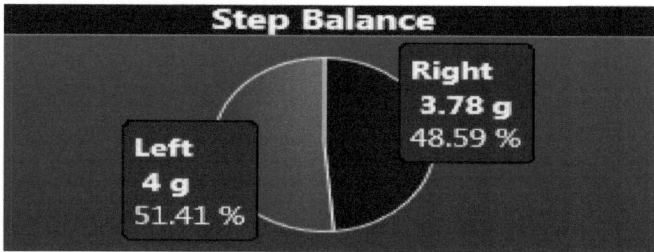

Figure 5: STATSports Step Balance Evaluation

(STATSports, 2016)

According to this pie chart, the staff is able to examine if a player subconsciously protects one of his feet by not transmitting full power in ground force reaction. Discrepancies from 10% up to 15% can indicate an incoming injury which can be prevented by reacting to these results and supply the player with an individual treatment to prevent possible injuries. STATSports also creates a so called "Fatigue Index", an algorithm comparing the workload of each player. This index provides the staff with important information about the individual vital status of a player and it can help to reduce the injury risk (STATSports, 2016).

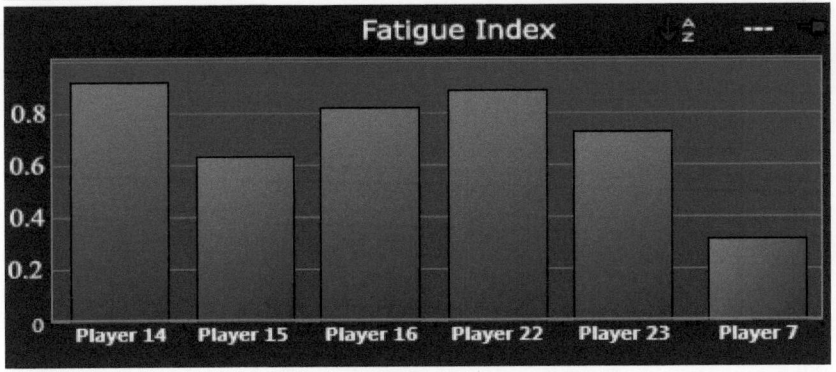

Figure 6: STATSports Fatigue Index
(STATSports, 2016)

Another feature in terms of injury prevention is the so called "Fingerprint Analysis" (STATSports, 2016) protocol, which creates an individual finger print for players, based on drills or activities during the training session. If a player is injured and on his way to be getting back to the team, the coaches are able to see how far his latest finger print in some drills and exercises differs from the finger prints when he was fully fit. This feature can give coaches an overview of the current fitness and rehabilitation level of players and whether they are ready to return to the team or not. Apart from the point of rehabilitation, the fingerprint analyses give coaches a general overview of individual players and their performance level, they are able to notice if players have increased or decreased in various training drills, so that they can change the training sessions for some players to get them back on track if their results have decreased (STATSports, 2016).

Another significant feature provided by the Viper system is the ability of implementing a fully detailed tactical analysis using the performance data of the players. This feature contains options like showing a positional and an activity heat map for all the players connected to the Viper Pod during a game or a training session. Other options are viewing session replays and synchronize recorded videos from specific training sessions.

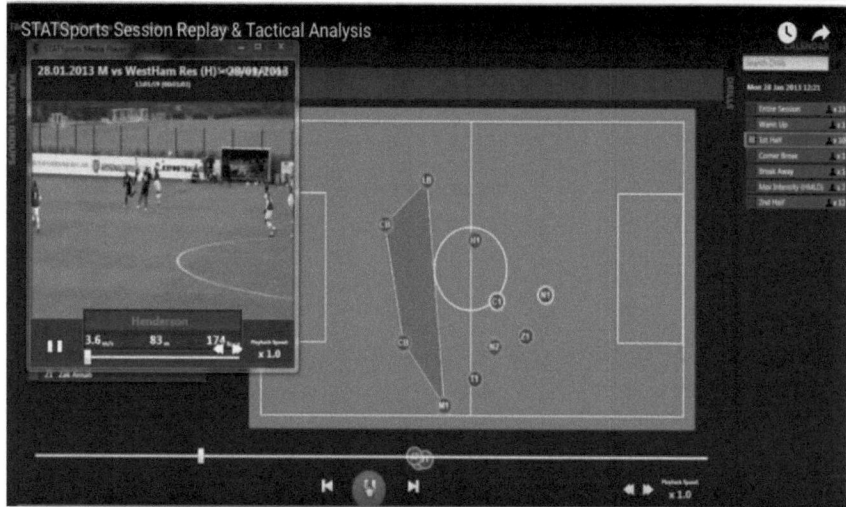

Figure 7: STATSports Session Replay & Tactical Analysis
(STATSports Youtube Channel, 2014)

As shown in this screenshot of a video published by STATSports, presenting the possible ways of various tactical analysis options, the coaching staff is able to combine these features provided by the Viper software to give a completely detailed overview over the players' performances and reactions in different situations of a game or training session like how players of the defensive line leave gaps or zones uncovered if the game shifts to the other side of the pitch and the whole team has to move their position. At the same time teams can use this against opponents by studying their movements in several situations and so coaches are able to work out the perfect game plan for various opponent teams individually. Another feature that goes into the direction of physical aspects and health of players is an application, included in the Viper system software, that lets the coaching staff get rates based on individual biomarkers received from saliva tests and perceived exertion by the players what they will fill into the application. This data will be downloaded automatically into the system so coaches are able to see how their players feel and how high the physical level is (STATSports, 2016).

Coming back to competitive features, the Viper system obviously provides tools to compare players' metrics individually in terms of various drills in training sessions. Bar charts allows a straight comparison of players on one metric at a time, so coaches are able to see which player in the team is the best one in specific metrics which can give conclusion about the players' overall abilities and on what some players have to focus in the training sessions. The Radar Graph provides the coaches with an overview of up to eight metrics at a time when observing drills in training sessions or specific players. With this tool, coaches are able to compare different metrics and various drills together to get a detailed picture of the current situation and on what to work on in future sessions to achieve the goals set (STATSports, 2016).

Through this summary about the STATSports Viper System, it became clear that this system is a highly developed and functional system that is able to provide a team's staff with nearly every information, data and metric they need, to analyze the performance of their players and to adapt the training sessions and game plans based on the evaluated to simply make the team and each player individually better by using highly developed wearable technology.

3.2.3 Professional use

STATSports Viper System is also a frequently used wearable performance tracking technology in the world of professional football. Over 40 European teams, a lot of MLS teams and even teams from New Zealand, Mexico, China and Dubai are using the Viper System on a regular basis in their training sessions. (STATSports, 2016) Among them is a large number of European top clubs, even 10 of the 32 competitors of the 2014 UEFA Champions League were STATSports clients (STATSports, 2014).

3.2.3.1 Arsenal FC

One of these ten UEFA Champions League starters is thirteen time English Premier League and twelve-time FA Cup winner Arsenal FC from London, United Kingdom. According to club doctor Gary O'Driscoll, working with STATSports Viper System brought players fitness and players welfare to the next level (STATSports, 2016). The Viper Pod sensors are being used in daily training sessions to measure individual player metrics like total distance, meters per minute, HML (high, middle, low) distance, high speed running, dynamic stress loads and sprints. (Arsenal FC & STATSports Technologies Ltd, 2013)

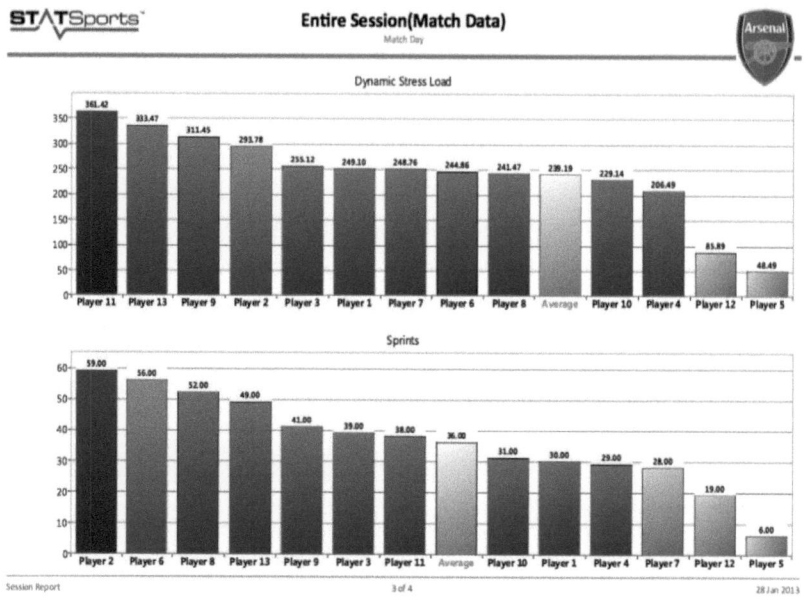

Figure 8: STATSports Arsenal FC training session data
(Arsenal FC & STATSports Technologies Ltd, 2013)

This extract of a session report of Arsenal FC supplied by STATSports shows several results in terms of dynamic stress load and sprints of thirteen different players compared to the average of them listed in a bar chart. Based on this chart, coaches are able to see which Arsenal player reaches the best metrics and which the worst, so the staff can create individual workout plans to get all the players on the same fitness and performance level. The same bar charts were also created for making measurements concerning total distance runs, meters per minute, HML distance, and high speed running for all thirteen players who wore the Viper Pod during this session.

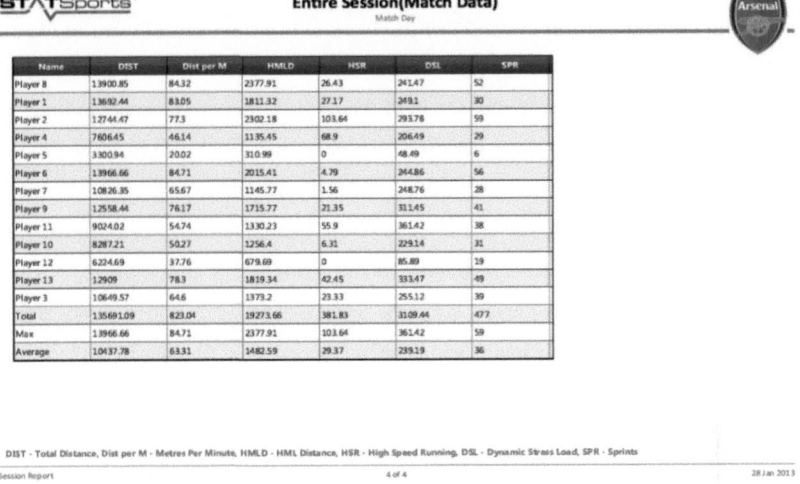

Name	DIST	Dist per M	HMLD	HSR	DSL	SPR
Player 8	13900.85	84.32	2377.91	26.43	241.47	52
Player 1	13692.44	83.05	1811.32	27.17	249.1	30
Player 2	12744.47	77.3	2302.18	103.64	293.78	59
Player 4	7606.45	46.14	1135.45	68.9	206.49	29
Player 5	3300.94	20.02	310.99	0	48.49	6
Player 6	13966.66	84.71	2015.41	4.79	244.86	56
Player 7	10826.35	65.67	1145.77	1.56	248.76	28
Player 9	12558.44	76.17	1715.77	21.35	311.45	41
Player 11	9024.02	54.74	1330.23	55.9	361.42	38
Player 10	8287.21	50.27	1256.4	6.31	229.14	31
Player 12	6224.69	37.76	679.69	0	85.89	19
Player 13	12909	78.3	1819.34	42.45	333.47	49
Player 3	10649.57	64.6	1379.2	23.33	255.12	39
Total	135691.09	823.04	19273.66	381.83	3109.44	477
Max	13966.66	84.71	2377.91	103.64	361.42	59
Average	10437.78	63.31	1482.59	29.37	239.19	36

DIST - Total Distance, Dist per M - Metres Per Minute, HMLD - HML Distance, HSR - High Speed Running, DSL - Dynamic Stress Load, SPR - Sprints

Session Report   4 of 4   28 Jan 2013

Figure 9: STATSports Arsenal FC training session data

(Arsenal FC & STATSports Technologies Ltd, 2013)

At the end of every training session, STATSports software provides the coaching staff with a summary of ever players' results of every tracked metric in form of a separate chart. Every individual player data is listed respectively to a specific training drill. Coaches are able to see entire session metrics of every player who was tracked during that training session thus they can create suitable workout plans to enhance the performance.

3.2.3.2 Liverpool FC

Another Premier League club and one of the clubs that have installed the STATSports Smart Training Ground System with fixed antennas around the training facility is Liverpool FC. The team benefitted strongly from using the Viper System which is the reason why they decided to install the Smart Training Ground System with fixed antennas instead of the mobile ones of the regular version of the STATSports Viper System (STATSport, 2016). Asked about the Smart Training Ground System in Liverpool, Ryland Morgans, Head Fitness and Conditioning Coach of the team said:

"STATSports Viper affects the way we train based on when we're using realtime it allows us to look at key metrics based on certain days of the week. It allows us to either reduce or

increase the amount of work players will do. The Smart Training Ground system allows us to make decisions while training is ongoing." (STATSports, 2016)

3.2.3.3 Juventus Turin

An example for a professional club outside of the English Premier League working with STATSports Viper System is Juventus Turin, the most successful club in Italian football with overall 61 titles. According to an interview of STATSport with Antonio Gualtieri, a member of the sports science department of Juventus Turin, the Italian club started working with the Viper System at the beginning of the 2014/2015 season on a regular basis (STATSport, 2015). Juventus players wore the STATSports Viper Pod in every training session except the day before a match and based on the gathered data during these training sessions, the sports science department developed and organized four different reports. One for the single session, one for the week from Monday to Sunday, another for the competitive week, which means from one match to the next match and a last one for the friendly matches. By organizing the training session reports like this, the staff was able to get an analysis for the entire team segmented by role and individual reference values to achieve all the goals they set to enhance the overall performance (STATSports, 2015). According to Gualtieri, the most important metric for the Juventus Turin staff, measured with the Viper System, was the High Metabolic Load Distance. This metric shows the total distance ran by a player, that was covered above an individual metabolic threshold which can be achieved through high speed running or explosive accelerations and decelerations in special training drills (STATSports, 2015).

3.2.3.4 FC Barcelona

Spanish La Liga champion of 2016 and the most popular football club alongside Real Madrid, FC Barcelona, is also a client of STATSports and works with their Viper System in training sessions to gather their players' performance data. (STATSports, 2016)

Figure 10: Lionel Messi wearing a STATSports vest during practice
(STATSports, 2015)

The players of the squad around Lionel Messi, who is shown in this picture during a training session wearing a STATSport Vest, are being tracked and monitored precisely by the coaching staff and besides getting enhancing their performance, the staff also used the Viper System to effectively prevent their players from getting injured during the season. Since starting to work with the STATSport Viper System, Barcelona's coaching staff obviously found the right methods based on the individual player data and metrics gathered with the Viper System to drastically reduce the number of serious injuries (reducing harmstring injuries to one comparing to nine last season), which was surely a key factor of their success in the league and on international duty (Williams, 2015).

Apart from these European top clubs and the other clubs mentioned earlier, also national teams trust in the benefits of the Viper System, which are the English, the Croatian, the Irish, the Northern Irish and the national team of the United States of America (STATSports, 2016).

3.3   Catapult Sports

Having stepped into the world of sports and the market of wearable sports technology in 2006, Australian public athlete analytics company Catapult Sports became the global leader in athlete analytics, providing teams of all forms of sports and leagues like the National Basketball Association (NBA), NFL and European top football leagues, with their products. (Catapult Sports, 2016) The devices produced by Catapult Sports were made to improve athlete performance as well as enable insight of in to athlete risk, readiness and return to play by providing the user with scientifically-validated player individual metrics (Catapult Sports, 2016). The product range of Catapult Sports includes wearable sensors, scientific analytic algorithms and athlete analytic platforms. In the following, the products designed for the use in football will be presented.

3.3.1   Components and functionality

3.3.1.1 OptimEye System

Catapult Sports developed the "OptimEye S5", a wearable sensor / monitor, placed between the shoulder blades of players wearing a vest belonging to it. The Australian company promotes the OptimEye S5 as very robust (military tested), comfortable to wear and as the thinnest monitor available (Catapult Sports, 2016). Additionally, Catapult Sports describes the OptimEye S5 as very precise, durable and simple to use.

Figure 11: Catapult Sports OptimEye S5
(Catapult Sports, 2016)

The OptimEye S5 captures movement and micro-movement metrics via a special type of navigation system, the global navigation satellite system (GNSS) (Catapult Sports, 2016). In addition, the OptimEye S5 is the only wearable tracking monitor to measure collisions of players during training sessions or games (Catapult Sports, 2016). Besides the OptimEye S5, Catapult Sports has developed a kind of light version of it, the OptimEye X4. Described as the "entry-level monitor" (Catapult Sports, 2016), the OptimEye X4´s subtle difference to the OptimEye S5 is lower the technical performance data and the size which is reduced by 40% (Catapult Sports, 2016).

Apart from these two sensors / monitors, Catapult Sports also developed the first wearable technology solely for goalkeepers, the "OptimEye G5". (Catapult Sports, 2016)

Figure 12: Catapult Sports OptimEye G5
(Catapult Sports, 2016)

Up to this, the tracking of goalkeeper performance in training sessions or games was limited to measurements of the heart rate. With the OptimEye G5, coaches and teams are now able to create individual "fingerprints" of their goalkeepers based on their individual performance (Catapult Sports, 2016). The OptimEye G5, also worn by goalkeepers like the OptimEye S5 and OptimEye X4 are worn by players included in vests, provides the coaching staff with data about the accurate number of dives including their intensity and direction during a session. In addition to this, data about jumps, accelerations, decelerations, changes of direction, repeat high intensity efforts, and time to recovery will be collected to be analyzed and evaluated by the coaching staff (Catapult Sports, 2016). All this evaluated data combined forms the individual fingerprint of a goalkeeper, that makes it able for a team to get valuable information about the individual goalkeeper performance and what could help to enhance this performance, that other traditional velocity measure methods generally cannot provide. All this gathered data from the OptimEye S5, the OptimEye X4 and the OptimEye G5 will be uploaded to the analytics platform developed by Catapult Sports called "Openfield" (Catapult Sports, 2016). Openfield gives coaches the opportunity to upload the data from their training sessions or games by plugging in up to 28 units or synchronize it wirelessly and then store all the data safely in the cloud to have access whenever and wherever the user needs it. With Openfield, Catapult Sports delivers an analytics platform with the highest degree of freedom in creating graphs, analytic reports and head to head comparisons without restrictions (Catapult Sports, 2016). The platform comes with pre-designed and often used analysis graphs and analysis charts in the segment of sports tracking, but the software makes it possible for the coaching staff to create every graph and chart they want to create in every individual way. For example, if a team splits up their training session in groups that work out different programs, exercises and training plans, Openfield gives coaches the opportunity to independently create analytic graphs, charts and reports for each of these groups (Catapult Sports, 2016). The advantage of evaluating individual groups independently is to analyze players based on their position or injury status (Catapult Sports, 2016). Adding to this, Openfield provides coaches with the opportunity to compare the latest data with data from previous training sessions or games. Furthermore, the software provides a wide range of comparison with prior data. Coaches are able to compare current data with data from last week, last month, the average evaluated data from the last twelve months, or even compare it with another players' metrics. In case of long term tracking, Openfield gives coaches a wide variety of possibilities to work with the data they gathered in their training sessions. Also in the field of bringing injured players back to training sessions, Openfield helps coaches and the coaching staff to avoid overhasty and unnecessary comebacks. By comparing the progress of the injured player with data evaluated prior to the injury, coaches can exactly recognize how the individual fitness level is and with which intensity the player is able to work out and move in training sessions. Another small but also helpful feature of the Openfield platform is the fact that coaches can choose to have their reports of individual players, group training sessions, or of the whole team performance automatically distributed through email to everyone they want, from assistant coaches over general managers to the medical staff, and wherever else needed (Catapult Sports, 2016). Also the safety of the teams' data is guaranteed by Catapult Sports. This is a very important aspect because teams are likely not to share their training performances with possible rivals. Catapult Sports promises the overall safety of data by storing them on the same servers as major banks do, so uploading and sharing individual data within the team seems risk-free (Catapult Sports, 2016).

3.3.1.2 GPSports

Apart from the OptimEye products by Catapult Sports, the company produces a wearable GPS tracking technology for players, the "SPI HPU", by acquiring Australian sports technology manufacturer "GPSports" in 2014 (Catapult Sports & GPSports, 2016).

The SPI HPU (High Performance Unit) is a wearable tracking technology, similar to the OptimEye products, but smaller in size and not that high functional. Advertised as an entry-level monitor, like the OptimEye X4, the SPI HPU allows the user to measure speed, distance, acceleration, deceleration, heart rate, running symmetry, collisions and metabolic powers individually for every player carrying the small sensor by wearing a similar vest as with the OptimEye products.

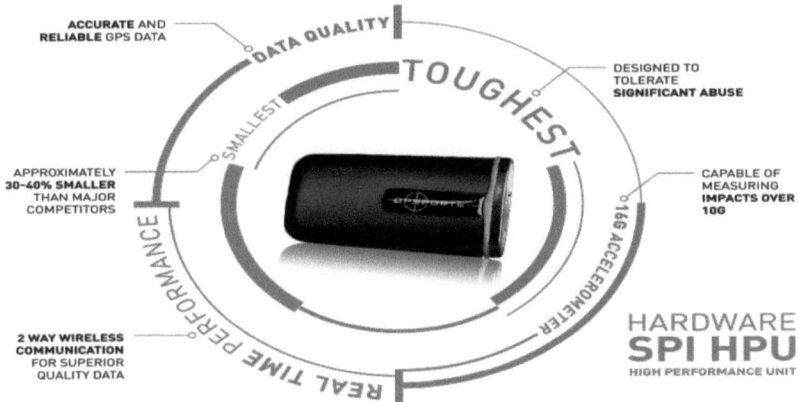

Figure 13: GPSports SPI IQ sensor
(GPSports, 2016)

The appendant software for the SPI HPU is called the "SPI IQ"(Catapult Sports & GPSports, 2016) As the Openfield platform by Catapult Sports, the SPI IQ is also fully customizable for coaches in terms of choosing between 30 graphs and 20 metrics to analyze and evaluate data with. Also similar to the OptimEye system, SPI IQ provides the coaches with the possibility to choose between analytic options like tracking the whole teams or position-dependent and further special groups of the team. Of course there is also the opportunity to compare individual players or groups of players' head to head to get exactly the information the coaches need to improve individual players and by doing this improving the team performance (Catapult Sports & GPSports, 2016). All in all, the SPI HPU together with its software and analytic platform, the SPI IQ provides coaches with almost the same data and possibilities to analyze and evaluate them as the products of the OptimEye System do, with the slight difference that the OptimEye System offers more specific ways of evaluating data and provides the user with a wider range of metrics to measure and in conclusion a more reliable data analysis.

3.3.2 Professional use

By providing nearly every sports team in the United States of America or Australia, whether it is football, American football, basketball or rugby, Catapult Sports made themselves a name in the market of wearable technology and are now providing hundreds of professional teams all over the world, including the top European leagues like English Premiear League, Italian Serie A, German Bundesliga or Spanish La Liga (Catapult Sports, 2016).

3.3.2.1 Leicester City

At the end of the 2015/2016 Premier League season, Leicester City, in the past a team battling relegation, surprisingly won the title after bringing a sensational season to a glorious end. A reason for their success clearly was the fact that the team of coach Claudio Ranieri suffered the fewest injuries of all teams in the league and for that reason, Ranieri was able to pick the same starting eleven for the majority of the season to keep a good rhythm. (Magowan, 2016) (Creasey, 2016).

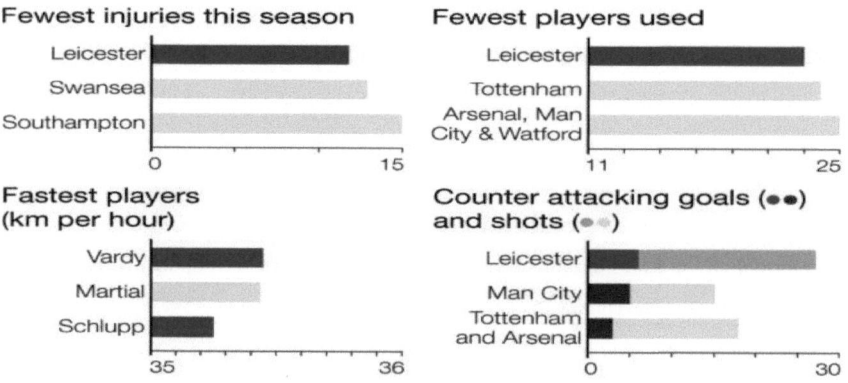

Figure 14: Leicester City season stats

(Magowan, 2016)

As shown in these diagrams by BBC, Leicester City were the team with the fewest injuries and fewest players used, ahead of top teams like Tottenham Hotspur, Arsenal and Manchester City, and were also best in the league in terms of counter attacking goals and having the fastest players in the squad, which is characteristic for their game plan relying on fast counter attacks with few passes that have won them the league title. The fact that Leicester City went through the season without major injuries was not only luck but also the daily work with wearable technology, like the OptimEye Products by Catapult Sport, in training sessions (Creasey, 2016). Leicester City uses the OptimEye S5 device across all first teams and the academy players of the club in their everyday training routine. The main reason why they used the Catapult Sports product was to check whether a player was ready to return from injury to the squad by comparing his individual data with data when he was fully fit so that the staff is able to examine how long it takes until the player is able to play again (Creasey, 2016). They did not only use the OptimEye S5 device to reduce injures, but also to improve their strength in playing fast counter attacks. By using the device, the coaching staff was able to see on which days the players needed recovery or a less intense training sessions, and on which days the squad was able to perform to its limits during a session. According to Matt Reeves, head of fitness and conditioning at Leicester City, on Thursdays after a training session, the squad lined up to perform 40 meter sprints to finish the training, which seems like a risky drill after an exhausting training session, but according to Reeves, the opposite was the case (Magowan, 2016). Another remarkable fact among professional teams is that Coach Claudio Ranieri often had the them be rested for 48 hours after games and even had a day off during the week, which is quite unconventional for professional football teams. However, by working with a lot technology especially the Catapult Sports products showed them that this is the right way to keep the players rested and fully fit to perform at the highest level, and maybe also above it, like in the 2015/2016 season (Magowan, 2016).

3.3.2.2 Newcastle United FC

Another English professional team, now relegated from the Premier League after the 2015/2016 season, but a big club with strong tradition, Newcastle United FC, is also a client of Catapult Sports. According to Jamie Harley, who works as sports scientist at Newcastle United FC, the club cannot see a time where they will not work with the devices (Catapult Sports, 2016).

The coaching staff at Newcastle organizes the training sessions in so called "micro-cycles", which means they try to replicate a training session which possibly had a positive effect on a game in the subsequent weeks (Catapult Sports, 2014). On a daily basis in training sessions, the coaching staff tracks how far players are running overall during that session using the Catapult Sports devices. They then individually evaluate the data and set individual goals concerning the maximum speed to achieve for every player. The main metric the staff regularly evaluates is the high intensity running data. By using these micro-cycles of training sessions and specifically monitoring them over and over, the staff is able to find out what has led to an injury and what parts had a really positive effect in order to enhance the individual performance (Catapult Sports, 2014). When a player incurred an injury, the staff was able to track down all the drills the player completed during recent training sessions by using the Catapult Sports devices to find out what led to that injury and to avoid doing them in the future. Also during the rehabilitation of players, before returning to the squad, the staff at Newcastle United FC worked with Catapult Sports devices to monitor the progress of the return by comparing new data with old data when the player was fully fit (Catapult Sports, 2014). According to Jamie Harley, Newcastle United FC made a lot of research to find the right wearable technology that fulfills all the needs of the coaching staff, so they eventually chose Catapult Sports because of its accuracy and reliability (Catapult Sports, 2014).

3.3.2.3 AC Milan

Former Italian Serie A champion, seven time Champions League winner and rival of Juventus Turin (using the STATSports Viper System) AC Milan is using Catapult Sports for some years now (Catapult Sports, 2016).

Like the other teams using Catapult Sports devices, the coaching staff of AC Milan is also trying to prevent injuries by monitoring individual player data to check what led to an injury. They are also controlling the return from injury by comparing individual data from specific drills. However according to the head of the athletic trainers at AC Milan, Bruno Dominici, there are many important aspects for the coaching staff when staff is monitoring the training session. The main aspect for them is to fully understand the needs of each individual player by evaluating several of different metrics to get a detailed overview (Catapult Sports, 2016). What they like about using Catapult Sports devices, as reported by Dominici, is that the staff is able to monitor a whole training session and gather individual information about metrics like player load, high intensity running and number of sprints, which is more important to them than just knowing about the total distance a player ran during a session (Catapult Sports, 2016).

3.3.2.4 Seattle Sounders FC

To return to the United States of America, where wearable technology is frequently used for years now in several sports and also in now football since the launch of the adidas miCoach system during the MLS All Star Game. MLS teams have also figured out for themselves which wearable technology system provides the highest added value for them and so the Seattle Sounders FC franchise chose to work with Catapult Sports (Catapult Sports, 2016). According to David Tenney, Sports Science and Performance Manager at the club, nearly every player of the squad is equipped with a wearable sensor by Catapult Sports during a training session. The main metric the staff around Tenney is monitoring during training sessions are the peak velocities each player individually achieves (Catapult Sports, 2016). The reason why this metric became their primary one is because of the data they receive, they are able to see how the intensity of training sessions affects players individually and so the staff is able to adapt the intensity to prevent injuries in training sessions (Catapult Sports, 2016). They also use the player load metric that, provided by the OptimEye system, which is based on individual accelerations of players to analyze the physical output.

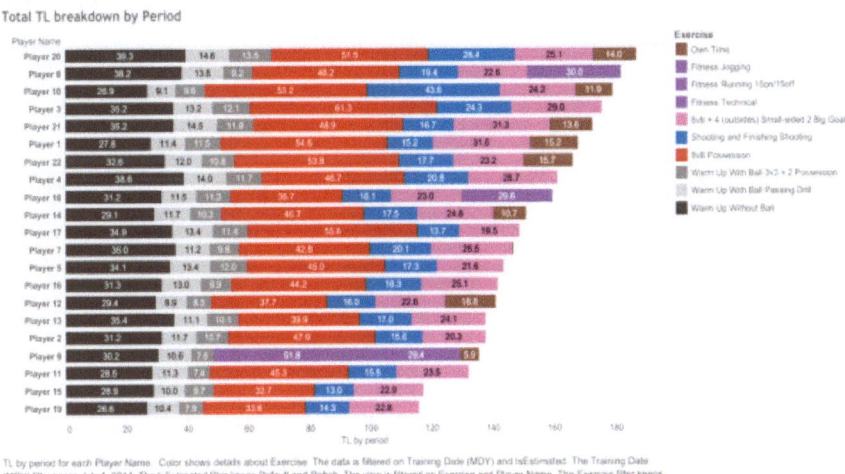

Figure 15: Seattle Sounders training session data

(Soper, 2014)

This diagram shows the gathered individual training load of some Seattle Sounders FC players who wore the Catapult Sports sensors during a training session. The training load is segmented between the several training drills like fitness jogging, fitness running, six against six on two goals, six against six with possession as main aspect, shooting drills and warm ups. Based on these output of individual training loads partitioned in these drills, the coaching staff is able to find out which drill was the most intense one for an individual player, which player achieved the best data and which player needs a different workout to maximize his statistics. Overall, the coaches are also able to see if the whole team needs a day off to recover, or if they intensify the drill intensity. The Seattle Sounders FC adjusted their training plan for a week to the evaluated and analyzed data of the OptimEye system by including a "non-impact recovery day" the day after a game (Catapult Sports, 2016). This day involves a 20-minute session on a spin bike, stretching, mobility and stability exercises to accelerate the recovery. For the second day after a game, the coaching staff is also able to adjust the intensity of the training session by using player data provided by the OptimEye system to see how fatigued the players still are (Catapult Sports, 2016). The way of using wearable technology like the Seattle Sounders do pays off. In 2014 they were analyzing more player data then ever and won most of their matches and were one of the few teams which was capable of performing at a high level late in the game when players have already lost a lot of energy. A third of their goals were scored in the last 15 minutes of a game, which shows how high the fitness level of the squad is, even they have at least one full day off per week (Soper, 2014).

3.4   Comparison of wearable technology systems

After the description of the three most popular and most used wearable technology systems, adidas miCoach Elite Team system, STATSports Viper System and Catapult Sports OptimEye system, and the exemplification of how several different professional football teams are using them, the following chapter compares the three different systems in terms of technical aspects and usage to get a final and compact overview about them.

3.4.1 Technical aspects

Table 1: Technical aspects of the three wearable devices

Company and product	adidas miCoach Elite Team System	STATSports Viper System	Catapult Sports OptimEye System
Number of components	5	3	4
Sensor weight	52 grams	< 50 grams	67 grams
Position tracking:	GPS	GPS	GNSS

(self-compiled, 2016)

The technical aspects of all three products are quite similar, except the number of components of each system. The adidas miCoach Elite Team System contains five components, the miCoach Elite Player Cell, the Techfit Elite, miCoach Elite Base, the miCoach Elite Dashboard and the miCoach Elite website (Donath, 2012). This system contains the most components, compared to Catapult Sports OptimEye System with four (OptimEye S5, OptimEye G5, Catapult Sports Vest and Software "Openfield") (Catapult Sports, 2016) and the STATSports Viper System with three components (Viper Pod, STATSports vest, Viper software). (STATSports, 2016) Also in terms of sensor weight, the difference is not that high, the adidas miCoach Player Elite Cell weighs about 52 grams (Nosowitz, 2012), the STATSports Viper Pod is slightly lighter with 50 grams (Williams, 2015) and the OptimEye S5 is the heaviest sensor with about 67 grams (Catapult Sports, 2016). In terms of how these devices are tracking the positions of players, only Catapult Sports uses the GNSS (Global navigation satellite system) (Catapult Sports, 2016), aiddas miCoach Elite Team System and STATSports Viper System are both using normal GPS (Global positioning system) (Vazquez, 2013) (STATSports, 2016).

3.4.2 Measured metrics

After a short summary and a comparison between the technical aspects of these three wearable technology performance tracking systems, this section focus on the functions of these three systems.

Table 2: Measured metrics from the three wearable devices

Company and product	Adidas miCoach Elite Team System	STATSports Viper System	Catapult Sports OptimEye System
Speed	✔	✔	✔
Training intensity	✔	✔	✔
Reaction speed	✔		
Distance	✔	✔	✔
Acceleration / Deceleration	✔	✔	✔
Jump height	✔		✔
Heart rate	✔	✔	✔
Sprints	✔	✔	✔
Dynamic stress load		✔	
High metabolic distance		✔	
Player collisions			✔
Goalkeeper metrics (dives, jumps)			✔

(self-compiled, 2016)

As shown in this table, every system of these three companies measures nearly the same metrics, there are only a few differences in some parts of measuring metrics. The Opti-mEye System by Catapult Sports is the only wearable technology device that is capable of tracking player collisions and specific metrics which are important for goalkeepers like the number and direction of jumps and dives (Catapult Sports, 2016). STATSports Viper System measures deeply in the field of intensity with measured metrics like dynamic stress load and high metabolic distance (STATSports, 2016). adidas miCoach Elite Team System`s unique selling point is the aspect that the device is capable to measure data like reaction speed jump height of players, if necessary (adidas, 2016).

To sum it all up, the difference between these three wearable technology devices in general is not that high from a technical and functional point of view. The reason why some teams prefer a certain wearable technology performance tracking system over another is mostly how convenient and nevertheless highly efficient the individual way of working with the provided data by using the included software and with it the technical, tactical and physical features and functions for the staff of the football team is.

4   Case study 1. FC Kalchreuth

In the subsequent chapter, the potential of wearable technology in amateur football will be tested by using wearable technology devices during training sessions of the Franconian amateur football club 1.FC Kalchreuth to see if an amateur club can benefit from using these devices in training sessions and if it makes sense for amateur clubs to purchase and use them in general.

4.1   General club information

1.FC Kalchreuth was founded in 1946 and is a club near Nuremberg that plays, apart from some youth teams, with two men´s team in the league system of Bavaria. The first team plays in the "Bezirksliga 1" which is overall the 7th highest league in Germany and the 4th highest league in Bavaria, the reserve team plays three leagues below in the "A-Klasse 8". Together, the two teams build a squad of 51 senior players that competes on a weekly basis in the Bavarian football league system.

Figure 16: Squad of 1.FC Kalchreuth 2016/2017
(self-compiled, 2016)

4.2   Training routine

The facility of 1.FC Kalchreuth includes two regular sized football fields and two smaller ones for youth teams or individual training sessions. During the preseason, the men´s teams of the club often have three to four training sessions per week, completing it with a friendly game on the weekend. During the season, which usually is from the end of July until the end of May, the squad usually practices two times per week, finishing the week with a league game on the weekend, mostly on Sunday. Typically, the two men´s teams practice separately at the same time, only if both squads are limited in players, they practice together. Like most of the clubs playing in a higher amateur league, the club also employs a physiotherapist to take care of injured or fatigued players. The focus and main aspects of training sessions and training drills during preseason and the regular season are well planned and structured for an amateur club. During the preseason the main goal of training sessions is to gain stamina by doing a variety of running drills with and without having a ball on the feet. During the regular season, the training sessions are structured to keep the squad in a rhythm by mixing strength and stamina drills to the drills with the focus on keeping the ball and creating a well-structured style of play by eliminating mistakes and weaknesses that came up during the preseason or recent games.

4.3　Used wearables in the Case Study

The three main products in terms of tracking performance data, adidas miCoach Elite System, STATSports Viper System and Catapult Sports OptimEye System are clearly designed for the use in professional sports as they would be way too expensive to be purchased by an amateur team and also almost no amateur team has the opportunity to work with a medical staff and sports scientists to evaluate data as complex as it would be. Because of these reasons, I chose devices that are less expensive but also less complex to work with my teammates to examine if there is potential for wearable technology in amateur football.

Two different devices were used, a wearable sensor, called "Pulse" by the company "Withings" and a smartwatch by Samsung called "Gear Live", to track data from ten players of my team and to interview them how they would rate the devices in terms of comfort, use, motivation and potential in amateur football. In terms of popularity and acquaintance about wearable technology, eight out of the ten interviewed players have heard of wearable technology in football in general, and seven of these eight have knowledge about the adidas miCoach Elite System, no one them has heard of STATSports Viper System nor Catapult Sports OptimEye Sytem.

4.3.1 Withings Pulse

The Withings Pulse is a small wearable sensor, worn by four teammates with a wristband during training sessions of about 90 minutes. With a price of 60€, the device is also afford-able for amateur teams with a low budget.

Figure 17: Withings Pulse sensor and wristband

(self-compiled, 2016)

The device is able to track activity as far as steps, intensity, calories burned, running dis-tance and total distance and also the individual heart rate. The device is controllable by touchscreen on the sensor and streams the measured data via Bluetooth to an app called "Withings" on a smartphone.

Figure 18: Withings phone application
(self-compiled, 2016)

As depicted in Figure 18 of the measured data from a teammate, the app displays the measured data in graphs and vivid form to make it easy to read off total distance, burned calories, steps and average heart rate.

4.3.2 Samsung Gear Live

The other device tested in training sessions of 1.FC Kalchreuth was the "Gear Live" smartwatch by Samsung, which is a smartwatch based on the android operating system and with a price of approximately 120€ located in a mid-range price segment.

Figure 19: Samsung Gear Live
(self-compiled, 2016)

Apart from having normal smartwatch features like access to the internet, messaging and maps by Google, the Samsung Gear Live comes with its own fitness tracking feature called "Fit" and makes it possible to track data like steps, total distance and heart rate. Six players of the squad used the smartwatch for about 45 minutes during a 90-minute training session.

4.3.3 Comparison and evaluation

As described, four out of ten players of the squad used the Withings Pulse sensor for a complete 90-minute training sessions and six out of ten players used the Samsung Gear Live smartwatch for 45 minutes per training session. The performance tracking process went over a period of two weeks (July 28th until August 11th) and because of the squad being in preseason, the training sessions were nearly identical structured in terms of types of exercises and drills. Starting with warm ups for about 20 minutes, the training sessions then were based on conditioning exercises with and without a ball on the feet. After that the major focus was on keeping possession of the ball in small areas followed by shooting practice and a competitive six against six or seven against seven game to finish the session.

4.3.3.1 Individual rating of the Withings Pulse sensor

The four players who used the Withings Pulse sensor device were from the age of 25 to 28 years and were between 183cm and 186cm tall. After using it for about 90 minutes and having metrics like distance, steps, intensity, burned calories and heart rate measured, the device was rated by them.

Table 3: Wearing comfort and usability of the Withings Pulse sensor

	1	2	3	4	5
COMFORT	✓✓✓	✓			
USABILITY		✓✓✓	✓		

(self-compiled, 2016)

After the training session the Withing Pulse sensor was individually rated in terms of wearing comfort during the session on a scale from 1 to 5. 1 meant the players did not notice the device at all during exercising, 5 meant they were heavily disturbed by it. As shown in this graphic, three out of four players rated the wearing comfort with a 1 which means there were no problems at all playing 90 minutes of football while wearing the sensor, only one teammate rated the device with a 2. The aspect of device usability was rated slightly inferior to the wearing comfort. Again this aspect was rated using a scale from 1 to 5 where 1 meant there were absolutely no problems with checking the stats during the session on the sensor itself and 5 meant the usability was a big problem for the players. Three out of four players rated the usability with a 2, only one with a 3. The sensor contains a button were the individual can scroll through the measured stats shown on the sensors display. A reason for rating this aspect not with the best grades would be the partly bad view to the display because of the wristband.

Table 4: Performance motivation by using the Withings Pulse sensor

	1	2	3	4	5
MOTIVATION	✓		✓✓		✓

(self-compiled, 2016)

The players were also asked if their motivation to perform better and with more intensity during a training session was higher because they knew their data would be measured by a wearable sensor. The motivation rating was also measured on a scale from 1 to 5 but this time 1 meant the motivation to perform more with more intensity did not increase at all by using a wearable sensor and 5 meant the player was highly motivated to perform at a higher level. Only one player said he was not motivated at all because he wore a wearable sensor tracking his performance, two player rated their motivation with a mediocre 3 and one player said he was highly motivated to perform better by wearing the device.

4.3.3.2 Individual rating of the Samsung Gear Live smartwatch

The remaining players, six out of ten from the age of 19 to 30 years and with a height of 176cm to 187cm, used the Samsung Gear Live smartwatch during 45 minutes of the 90-minute training session, that tracks individual metrics like distance, heart rate and steps. The rating factors for the Samsung Gear Live smartwatch were the same like the rating of the Withings Pulse Sensor.

Table 5: Wearing comfort and usability of the Samsung Gear Live smartwatch

	1	2	3	4	5
COMFORT	✓✓✓	✓✓	✓		
USABILITY	✓	✓✓✓	✓		

(self-compiled, 2016)

As shown in table 5, the overall comfort was mostly positively seen by the players as three of them rated the wearing comfort with the top grade of 1 out of 5, two players gave a 2 and only one gave a 3 because the smartwatch felt massive on the arm while playing football. In terms of usability the Samsung Gear Live smartwatch received also overall positive but not perfect ratings. Four out of six rated the usability with a 2 out of 5, only one gave the top grade 1 and only one the mediocre grade 3.

The group that used the Samsung Gear Live smartwatch were also asked about whether they were more motivated in performing better and with more intensity while wearing the wearable smartwatch. Just like the Withings Pulse sensor, the rating was based on a scale from 1 o 5 where 1 meant they were not more motivated at all and 5 meant the players were extremely motivated to perform better while getting their performance tracked.

Table 6: Performance motivation by using the Samsung Gear Live smartwatch

	1	2	3	4	5
MOTIVATION	✓✓✓		✓✓	✓	

(self-compiled, 2016)

Compared with the Withings Pulse sensor, the influence of the smartwatch to the individual player motivation was almost nonexistent. Three out of six players stated they were not more motivated at all to perform with more intensity, two players chose to rate their motivation with a mediocre 3 and only one player gave a 4 and said he was more motivated by wearing the smartwatch and knowing his performance would be tracked by the device.

4.4 Possibilities for amateur teams

By using devices like the Withings Pulse sensor or the Samsung Gear Live smartwatch, amateur teams get the opportunities to control training effort. Not as specific as professional teams do by using the professional and expensive products, but specific enough to efficiently improve their players with less complex methods and no highly developed sports science knowledge. Coaches of amateur clubs get the opportunity to compare the total running distance of players during a training session and see afterwards which player lacks condition and which player is already in great shape, especially in preseason this gives the coach of an amateur team an interesting overview of his squad and the fitness level.

Figure 20: Two separate training sessions tracked by the Withings Pulse sensor

(self-compiled, 2016)

During the performance tracking of 1.FC Kalchreuth, on August 2nd, one player recorded a total running distance of 6,94 kilometers, two days later during the training session on August 4th another player run 9,92 kilometers in total. Only by having these two metrics, a coach is able to see which training session was more intense and which player performed at a high level this particular week. Apart from adapting training sessions to running performance of individual players, coaches of amateur teams can also use the heart rate tracking feature of both the Withings Pulse sensor and the Samsung Gear Live smartwatch to control training intensity of training sessions with less complex methods.

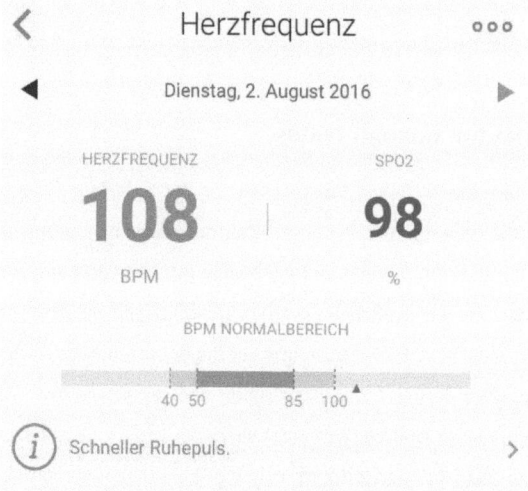

Figure 21: Heart rate measured with the Withings Pulse Sensor
(self-compiled, 2016)

As shown in Figure 21 from the Witings Pulse sensor app, the sensor provides the player with the measured heart rate during the activity, coaches can easily notice how intense different exercise drills are for individual players and can adapt the length of breaks between drills to the level of the heart rate of players to reduce the risk of injuries during long high intensity preseason condition drills.

5 Conclusion

As described above, the difference between professional football teams and amateur teams is obvious, especially in terms of specific feature opportunities to adapt training sessions to individual needs and team needs to improve the whole squad purposefully. Most of the amateur teams have not the financial budget nor the required personal and technical knowledge to purchase and use efficiently a professional performance tracking system. Besides this fact, amateur teams only train two to three times a week and football is not a main profession, so it is also difficult to set specific and ambitious training session goals like professional clubs. However, with less expensive and less complex wearable technologies, amateur teams may be able to connect amateur football with technology and performance tracking. By purchasing low priced wearable devices like the Withings Pulse sensor, amateur teams are able to track the individual training session of each players and to improve their performance in the long run. Indeed, the measured data is not as highly complex and informative like the professional performance tracking wearables like adidas miCoach Elite System, STATSports Viper System or Catapult Sports OptimEye System. However, the data provided by these wearables is sufficient to improve training sessions and to create different workout drills on an amateur level. Furthermore, no amateur team has sufficient medical personal to monitor the individual physical condition of players to prevent injuries or notice what their body needs in detail. By using wearable technology that measures metrics like the heart rate, amateur teams are able to monitor cost-efficiently at least some parts of their players' health

In summary, it can be stated that wearable technology definitely has a potential in amateur football. Although amateur teams will not be able to get access to the wide range of features provided by professional wearable technology, because of the lack of funds to work with high-end wearable devices and highly qualified sports scientists or medical experts, amateur teams have the chance to use cost-efficiently wearable devices to increase their overall performance. It does not require great effort or special knowledge to use these affordable wearable devices in the right way to adapt training sessions to gain overall efficiency in training drills and individual performance of amateur players. For amateur teams it surely is profitable to invest effort, money and time in integrating wearable devices into their training sessions, not only to make it more efficient for both individual and team performance, but also to monitor physical health of players, a relevant aspect a lot of amateur teams do not attach great importance to. To include wearable technology entirely into amateur football, amateur teams need to be enlightened about the advantages and possibilities wearable technology provides, as most of them do not know anything about them and how to benefit from using them. After getting to know the advantages and the easy use of these wearable technologies, my club considers to purchase some devices to test them for a longer period and to conceivably integrate them into the normal training sessions. If only more amateur clubs get the chance to be informed about the opportunities of wearable technology, it probably will not take as much time as expected to have these devices used in weekly training sessions of amateur clubs.

References

adidas. (2016). miCoach Smart Ball. *adidas Online Shop*. Retrieved from

http://www.adidas.de/micoach-smart-ball/G83963.html

adidas. (2016). miCoach X_Cell und Textilgurt. *adidas Online Shop*. Retrieved from

http://www.adidas.de/micoach-x_cell-und-textilgurt/Z51350.html

Arsenal FC, & STATSports Technologies Ltd. (2013). Entire Session (Match Data)
    Entire Session (Match Data).

Brüggen, O., Hübner, W., & Nationalmannschaft, D. (2014). *Deutsche
    Nationalmannschaft trainiert mit adidas miCoach Elite Team System.*

Catapult Sports. (2014). Newcastle United FC mastering Catapult. *Catapult Sports
    Youtube Channel.* Retrieved from https://www.youtube.com/watch?v=ikNUv-OMfKs

Catapult Sports. (2016). Smarter, stronger, sleeker.

Catapult Sports, & GPSports. (2016). *SPI HPU, SPI IQ.*

Catapult Sports. (2016). About. *Catapult Sports*. Retrieved from

http://www.catapultsports.com/about/

Catapult Sports. (2016). Outdoor. *Catapult Sports*. Retrieved from

http://www.catapultsports.com/system/outdoor/

Catapult Sports. (2016). Find your Football Fingerprints. *Catapult Sports*. Retrieved from

http://www.catapultsports.com/sports/football/

Catapult Sports. (2016) Your First Athlete Analytics Platform. *Catapult Sports*. Retrieved
    from http://www.catapultsports.com/system/openfield/

Catapult Sports. (2016). Clients. *Catapult Sports*. Retrieved from

http://www.catapultsports.com/clients/clients/

Catapult Sports. (n.d.) Catapult acquires GPSports. *Catapult Sports*. Retrieved from
http://www.catapultsports.com/de/medien/catapult-acquires-gpsports/

Catapult Sports. (2016) AC Milan. *Catapult Sports.* Retrieved from

http://www.catapultsports.com/us/clients/case-studies/ac-milan/

Catapult Sports. (2016). Seattle Sounders FC. *Catapult Sports.* Retrieved from http://www.catapultsports.com/us/clients/case-studies/seattle-sounders/

Costello, B. (2012). Lies, damn lies, and statistics: How adidas' miCoach could change MLS (plus a cameo from Jean-Baptiste). *Portland Timbers.* Retrieved from http://www.timbers.com/post/2012/09/04/lies-damn-lies-and-statistics-how-adidas-micoach-could-change-mls-plus-cameo-jean

Creasey, S. (2016). Data analytics paved way for Leicester win. *Computerweekly.com*, 4–8.

Donath, A. (2012) Fußballer Herzfrequenz vom Platz direkt aufs Trainer-iPad, *Golem.* Retrieved from

http://www.golem.de/news/adidas-micoach-elite-fussballer-herzfrequenz-vom-platz-direkt-aufs-trainer-ipad-1207-93352.html

González, Z.D., FIFA World Cup is also in for Wearables. *Wearable Technologies.* Retrieved from https://www.wearable-technologies.com/2014/06/fifa-world-cup-is-also-in-for-wearables/

Hymers, M. (2014). In a bid to win the World Cup: DFB team makes the most of cutting edge technology. *adidas Group.* Retrieved from

http://blog.adidas-group.com/2014/07/in-a-bid-to-win-the-world-cup-dfb-team-makes-the-most-of-cutting-edge-technology/

Johnson, D. (2015). Top smart gadgets for soccer/football. *Gadgets & Wearables.* Retrieved from http://gadgetsandwearables.com/2015/12/25/top-smart-gadgets-for-footballsoccer/

MLS Communications. (2012). MLS, adidas to launch first "smart soccer league" in 2013. *MLS Soccer.* Retrieved from http://www.mlssoccer.com/post/2012/07/19/mls-adidas-launch-first-smart-soccer-league-2013

Magowan, A. (2016). Leicester City: The science behind their Premier League title. *BBC.* Retrieved from http://www.bbc.com/sport/football/36189778

Neal, R.W. (2013). Smart Soccer: MLS, Chelsea FC Using Adidas Wearable Technology To Improve Training. *International Business Times.* Retrieved from http://www.ibtimes.com/smart-soccer-mls-chelsea-fc-using-adidas-wearable-technology-improve-training-1360145

Nosowitz, D. (2012). The adidas miCoach will track real-time data from every single MLS player. *Popular Sciene.* Retrieved from

http://www.popsci.com/technology/article/2012-07/adidas-micoach-will-track-real-time-data-every-single-mls-player

Plummer, L. (2016). Super Bowl 50: How wearable tech is changing the NFL. *Wareable.* Retrieved from http://www.wareable.com/sport/super-bowl-2016-50-wearable-tech-in-the-nfl

Soper, T. (2014). How the Sounders use wearables to improve soccer player fitness, with help from tableau. *GeekWire.* Retrieved from

http://www.geekwire.com/2014/sounders-tableau/

Soper, T. (2015). How the German national team used wearable technology to win the World Cup. *GeekWire.* Retrieved from http://www.geekwire.com/2015/german-national-soccer-team-used-wearable-technology-win-world-cup/

STATSports. (2014) STATSports Session Replay & Tactical Analysis. *STATSports Youtube Channel.* Retrieved from

STATSports. (2014) STATSports Viper within the Champions League. *STATSports.* Retrieved from http://statsports.com/statsports-viper-within-champions-league/

https://www.youtube.com/watch?v=edZMpQSURMs

STATSports. (2015, July 5). An all sports Champions League final. *STATSports.* Retrieved from http://statsports.com/statsports-champions-league-final/

STATSports. (2015, September 9). Exclusive Interview: Sports science at Juventus FC - Antonio Gualtieri. *STATSports.* Retrieved from http://statsports.com/exclusive-sport-science-juventus-fc-antonio-gualtieri/

STATSports. (2016). Viper Pod. *STATSports.* Retrieved from

http://statsports.com/technology/viper-pod/

STATSports. (2016). Clients. *STATSports.* Retrieved from http://statsports.com/clients-2/#clients

STATSports. (2016). Viper Software. *STATSports.* Retrieved from http://statsports.com/technology/viper-software/

Svetlik, J. (2015, August 7). It's coming home: How wearable tech is about to change football. *Wareable.* Retrieved from http://www.wareable.com/fitness-trackers/how-wearable-tech-is-about-to-change-football

Vazquez, S. (2013, August 15) Adidas miCoach Elite System Provides Trainers and Players with Real-Time Performance Metrics. *Sport Techie.* Retrieved from http://www.sporttechie.com/2013/08/15/adidas-micoach-elite-system-provides-trainers-and-players-with-real-time-performance-metrics/

Williams, C. (2015). Just for kicks - Viper Pod. *Seminoles.* Retrieved from http://www.seminoles.com/ViewArticle.dbml?ATCLID=209884000

Williams, K. (2015, April 22) The Stats Vest and the injury-free Barcelona. *Grup 14.* Retrieved from https://grup14.com/article/the-stats-vest-and-the-injury-free-barcelona

Appendix

This is the template for the interview questions answered by 1.FC Kalchreuth players – the results were handed in separately.

Interview Wearable Technology 1. FC Kalchreuth

Age:

Height:

Weight:

1. To introduce you to the topic, there are well known products in the wearable technology market used by professional football teams, have you heard of wearable technology in football at all?

   ☐ Yes

   ☐ No

2. If yes, one of these three? (Multiple Choice)

☐ adidas miCoach

☐ STATSports Viper System

☐ Catapult Sports Optim Eye

3. In the last training session, which wearable technology have

you used?

☐ Withings Sensor   ☐ Smartwatch

4. How was the overall wearing comfort during the session?
Please tick the appropriate box (1= didn't noticed it at all; 5=
disturbed in my movement)

☐ 1   ☐ 2   ☐ 3   ☐ 4   ☐ 5

Something else?

5. **How would you describe the level of usability? Was it easy or hard to use the device (1= really easy to use, no problems; 5= big problems, no idea how to use it)**

☐ 1 ☐ 2 ☐ 3 ☐ 4 ☐ 5

Something else?

6. **Were you motivated to perform with higher intensity by using it? (1= not at all, 5= really eager to perform at a higher level)**

☐ 1   ☐ 2   ☐ 3   ☐ 4   ☐ 5

Something else?